THE BOOK OF BALANCE

LAO TZU'S *TAO TEH CHING*

DEAR MICHAEL

IN CELEBRATION OF
OUR SHARED VISION

TAOSHIKO
玄咨

Dear Michael,

THE BOOK OF BALANCE

LAO TZU'S *TAO TEH CHING*

A NEW TRANSLATION

BY

YASUHIKO GENKU KIMURA

PARAVIEW
Special Editions

New York

The Book of Balance was originally published by the University of Science and Philosophy in 2002.

Cover art and interior design by Vince Lee, Contact Printing
Cover design by smythtype
ISBN: 1-931044-90-2
Library of Congress Catalog Number: 2004103619

CONTENTS

Dedicated to the Sages of the world
who throughout the ages
have kept timeless wisdom alive.

FOREWORD

The Logos of Tao:
Translating the *Tao Teh Ching* in a Global Age

Ashok K. Gangadean, Ph.D.

Upon entering the 21st Century and facing an unprecedented global age, two powerful themes have emerged which challenge any attempt to authentically render an ancient classical text such as the *Tao Teh Ching*. One is the recognition that every translation is also, at the same time, an interpretation that is shaped and colored by the worldview, mental ecology, or interpretive lens of the translator. This vital consideration brings into sharp relief the challenge of interpreting and translating across widely diverse worldviews, ideologies, cosmologies, or cultural perspectives. If the translator is lodged within a particular cultural ecology or worldview, there is an obvious challenge to gain sufficient critical distance from and access to the indigenous worldview and conceptual ecology of the text or script being translated. How is it possible to translate authentically across diverse worldviews?

The second theme, which provides a vital clue to answering this question, is the recognition that there is and must be a Primal Logos that is the common ground and generative source of diverse worldviews, perspectives, and cultural traditions. This theme is distilled from a long tradition of perennial philosophy that has now matured with the maturation of global reason. This powerful theme suggests that when we step back from any particular worldview or cultural lens and enter a truly global perspective where diverse worldviews and traditions co-originate and arise, a global horizon opens wherein it becomes more evident that there is a Primal First Principle, a Primal Infinite Word or Unifying Field that is the common global source of diverse worldviews, scripts, perspectives and forms of life.

In crossing into this global perspective it becomes more evident that this fundamental Logos is essentially global in scope and power, and as the common ground of diverse worlds, is a key to authentic translation and interpretation across worldviews and textual traditions. Indeed, this global perspective and global Logos reveal that there has been a latent global tradition of diverse scripts and texts through the ages which co-express this Infinite Word in diverse creative ways. Here it becomes evident that the global power of this Logos is the key to translating and interpreting across diverse worldviews.

In this brief Foreword I would like to focus on these two themes (which are developed more systematically and in depth elsewhere) and indicate why I believe this excellent translation of the *Tao Teh Ching* by Yasuhiko Kimura meets the highest standards of philosophical translation and is an important contribution to Global Philosophy. I shall make clear that this classical Chinese script is a powerful expression of the Primal Logos that is the common source of great scripts across philosophical and cultural traditions through the ages. For this reason, making clear the **Tao of Logos** and the **Logos of Tao** will help to bring out the global and perennial power of this classical text, and make clear why this script has profound relevance for today's readers facing the challenges of life in a global age.

Entering a Global Perspective: The Logos of Tao

As we enter a global age where diverse worldviews are increasingly in intensified encounters it is of the utmost importance to cultivate a global awareness wherein diverse worldviews and cultural perspectives may mutually engage in authentic dialogue. But entering this expanded global consciousness calls forth profound transformations in how we conduct our minds. And we shall soon see that the *Text of Tao* essentially addresses and invokes such expanded rational awareness. So how do we cross from our more localized perspectives and mental lenses into this global lens?

It is found that when we stand back from any one cultural, philosophical, or disciplinary orientation and cross into the **global perspective** where widely variant worldviews originate and intersect, striking patterns emerge that are not as readily seen (perhaps can't be seen) from more localized narrative forms of life. In this global space of diverse cosmologies and grammars of reality it is found, for example, that diverse worldviews through the ages have gravitated to some Ultimate First Principle or Presiding Reality that is the source of its form of life.

This **global transformation** taps a deeper **inter-perspectival dimension** of rational consciousness, and it becomes apparent that the vast spectrum of diverse cultural and philosophical narrative attempts through the ages to name and express "What is First" converge on the same Primal Infinite Source. For example, the discourse of *TAO* in classical Chinese thought is one magnificent attempt at "First Philosophy"—the enterprise of developing a grammar and narrative to express the most fundamental Reality. Again, the grammar of *AUM* in the Hindu Vedic tradition is another example of this quest for the primal universal grammar.

This is certainly true of the Judaic biblical script as it seeks to name the Infinite First Principle—*YAHWEH*; and this tradition unfolds in the emergence of Christianity in its attempt to express an ultimate narrative in the form of *The Infinite Word* and *Christ*, and in the birth of Islam as it seeks to express the Primal Name of *ALLAH*, and so on. Ranging further, it is clear that in the development of Buddhist thought the radical attempt to disclose ultimate truth as beyond all names and forms, as *SUNYATA*—Absolute Emptiness—likewise qualifies as an alternative grammatical strategy in approaching What-is-First.

And, of course, it is no accident that a continuing deep drive throughout the birth and evolution of European philosophy since Greek origins to express the fundamental Logos, to uncover the missing primal Logic, to tap the missing universal grammar of

Logos is yet another great chapter in this perennial and global quest to express what is Ultimate. This certainly appears in the striving of the sciences to uncover the fundamental laws and patterns of the Universe, to name and express the "Ultimate Stuff"— be it "Energy," "Force," "First Cause," or Nature.

For our purposes here in inquiring into the global source and resource of interpretation and translation across and between worldviews, it is essential to acknowledge that these diverse narratives of the Ultimate Ground are alternative co-expressions of *What-is-First*. This can only become clear in entering the multi-perspectival and inter-perspectival rational space of the **global perspective**. For in crossing into this higher-order dimension of global consciousness there is a "dilation" of rational awareness and a profound "inversion" of perspectivity into an Integral, Nondual, and Holistic dynamic of minding (a Primal Logic) that reveals that the Infinite First is and must be the same generative source of all realities—of all perspectives, all worldviews, all cosmologies, grammars, narratives, disciplines, of all experience. This suggests that a qualified translator of a Logos Script, such as the *Tao*, must have competence and be literate in the global grammar of Logos.

Indeed, in crossing into this **global rational space** and technology or logistic of minding, another striking pattern becomes evident. It becomes clear that diverse First Narratives — East, West and other—converge toward a **global consensus** that we **humans are as we mind**—our experience, our lifeworlds, our cultural identities, our disciplinary narratives, the phenomena that make up our living realities are all profoundly co-shaped by our thought processes, by how we conduct our mind. And a potent global theme across worldviews recognizes that humans tend to become lodged, ensnared, obsessed, blocked, and locked into **egocentric or monocentric patterns** of minding or processing reality that have devastating consequences for the human condition and are the common source of existential and rational pathologies of all sorts. This theme resonates throughout the *Tao*.

This profound rational theme—*that we are as we mind*—brings into sharp relief the method, logistic, or technology of "minding" as being of ultimate importance. It becomes clear that "egocentric" patterns of minding reality typically separate the thinking subject from the "object" of what-is-thought, perceived, or experienced. In thus objectifying all that appears to its consciousness egocentric reason proceeds to "package" and "process" all phenomena, including itself, in artificially constructed language, classifications, and categorizations that inevitably deform whatever appears. And egocentric minding typically tends to be "monocentric" (rather than dialogic), processing its world from its own reductive perspective, ideology, worldview, or narrative form of life. This tendency to privilege one's own worldview or localized lens is one of the primary flaws in approaching a text like the *Tao*.

In this way, any and every worldview, ideology, discipline, or narrative (whatever the content) that is processed in egocentric thought patterns will share the same deep structural rational and existential pathologies. This global perspective also makes clear that there are diverse alternative strategies to advance beyond egocentric reason toward the integral and hologistic dynamics of global reason. Indeed, it becomes evident that the great philosophical and spiritual teachings of the ages all converge on this common rational prescription—that the key to human flourishing and to the authentic encounter with Reality comes with this overcoming of the adolescent and dysfunctional habits of egocentric minding and maturing into the integrative, nondual, and dialogical patterns of natural global reason.

It is of the highest importance for us in the present context of exploring the conditions of authentic translation and interpretation that we bring into the open the distortions of the egocentric lens. An authentic translation of the *Tao* must step back from the egocentric lens and enter a holistic and integral mental lens that expresses the *Logos of Tao*.

It becomes clear in crossing into the global lens that there is a **Primal Logic** of **What-is-First**, and in my earlier work in developing **global first philosophy** I have suggested that it would help accelerate research, understanding, the rational enterprise and cultural advancement for planetary well-being to introduce a global name for this *Primal Word* to help humanity recognize more clearly a recurrent global insight that the *Primal Infinite Principle* must be one and the same generative source of all worldviews, perspectives, cultures, traditions, disciplines, narratives, and first philosophies. And I have proposed *Logos* (taken from Greek classical attempts to tap the ultimate structure and dynamics of natural reason and discourse) as such a **global name** to help remind us that there is, after all, a fundamental Universal Grammar or Logic of the Infinite Word which is the universal rational context for all discourse and experience.

Thus I am suggesting that the *Tao Teh Ching* is best placed in this global perspective as a wonderful and classical rendering of this global Logos. This means, of course, that the *Tao* is integral to a global tradition of diverse Logos scripts and illuminates the Primal Word in unique and powerful ways. It deepens and further illuminates the Grammar of Logos.

Translating the Tao: Competence and Qualifications

We have been suggesting that it takes a global consciousness to render adequately a global script such as the text of *Tao*. It is of the utmost importance that the translator have a true understanding of the script, the philosophical imagination to commune with it, and the philosophical grammar to render it.

Yasuhiko Genku Kimura is eminently qualified to present us with a philosophically sensitive and insightful translation of this rich and illusive text. His years of training and experience in the meditative arts are invaluable in gaining depth and literacy in the global grammar of Logos. And his extensive work in seeking to integrate Western science with Eastern philosophy further adds to his qualifications in the integral and holistic logic of the Unified Field which plays out in the Logos of *Tao*. Kimura is keenly aware of the dynamic of egocentric thought patterns and his rich experience in the integral logic and thought patterns of the Unified Field places him in a unique position to open new depths to the *Tao*.

There are numerous translations available in the marketplace, but this one stands out for me in its conceptual lucidity, philosophical accessibility and textual fidelity. The Logos of the text is beautifully rendered without sacrificing the poetics. The spiritual gems of this great perennial text shine forth for the reader in a global light. This is an important contribution to global philosophy which taps the global power of the *Tao*.

Ashok K. Gangadean, Ph.D.
Professor of Philosophy, Haverford College

TRANSLATOR'S NOTE

1. TAO

Understanding the Undefinable

TAO TEH CHING begins with the statement: *The Tao Eternal is beyond definition. No name given can capture its eternality.*

This statement can be translated more literally: *The Tao that can be defined is not the Eternal Tao. The Name that can be assigned is not the Eternal Name.*

The same statement can also be translated more hermeneutically: *The Tao that is atemporally abiding cannot be reduced to any finite description or predication in language. The naming in language that is temporal and finite cannot capture the atemporally abiding Tao in its atemporal abidingness.*

Thus, no matter how one translates this statement, the undefinable and unnamable nature of the Tao remains explicitly clear. However, this does not mean that the Tao is beyond comprehension. The Tao is comprehensible, communicable, and applicable. The eighty-one passages of *Tao Teh Ching* individually and as a whole provide us with the powerful and thorough understanding of the Tao—assuming that we know how to read this classical text and how to understand the undefinable. The question therefore is how to understand that which is *by definition* undefinable.

A Unique Feature of the Sinic Thought

Reading *TAO TEH CHING* and other classical Chinese texts requires an understanding and innerstanding of the unique features of the Sinic Mind, which is different from both the Western Mind and the Indic Mind.

In general, what characterizes the Western Mind is its proclivity for the ordered, the rational, and the male with an aversion or suspicion of the non-ordered, the intuitive, and the female. The Western Mind's main theme has been the transformation of chaos (non-order) into cosmos (order). Therefore, throughout the history of Western thought and culture, the primary value has been placed upon reason, rationality, and linear logic. For the Western Mind, Reality is rational and should be comprehensible through rational means.

By contrast, what generally characterizes the Indic Mind is its proclivity for the mystical that transcends order, rationality, and linear logic. The Indic Mind's main theme has been the transcendence from cosmos (mundane order) to chaos (transcendental mystery). The Indic Mind, in its advanced state, is trans-rational and supra-logical, which, while remaining supremely rational and logical—Indians are great mathematicians and logicians—uses logic and rationality mainly to point toward that which transcends logic and rationality. For the Indic Mind, Reality is transrational and can be understood only through our "mystical union" with it.

To the Sinic Mind, as the *yin-yang* symbol represents, cosmos and chaos, order and non-order, rationality and transrationality, the male and the female are complementary, and their coupling interplay constitutes the essential dynamics of life and the universe. Therefore, the main theme of the Sinic Mind and Thought has been the attainment of balance or balanced complementarity between the ordered and the non-ordered, the rational and the transrational, the physical and the metaphysical, and the male and the female. In the Sinic culture, the primary value is placed upon creating and maintaining balance and harmony between the opposites. For the Sinic Mind, Reality is both rational and transrational, and should be understood through the complementary workings of reason and intuition.

By way of contrast, of the two greatest sages of antiquity, Confucius' teaching focuses on how to attain balance and harmony in society, where diverse and opposing forces dynamically interact to often create discord and conflict, while Lao Tzu's teaching focuses on how to attain balance and harmony between the inner and the outer dimensions of human life through the attainment of inner balance and harmony in accordance with the immutable principles of the Tao, dynamically manifesting in Nature within and without.

Ultimately, the term Tao points to the same Reality or Being to which the terms Logos (Greek) and Brahman (Sanskrit) point. However, while Logos designates the Ordering Logic aspect and Brahman the Primordial Dynamic aspect, Tao signifies the Integral Balance aspect of this Reality. Whereas Logos led the Western civilization to the physics of the outer universe and Brahman led the Indic civilization to the metaphysics of the inner universe, Tao led the Sinic civilization to the ethics of both the outer and inner worlds, of both this world and the other.

Reading the *Tao Teh Ching*

Therefore, to read and to comprehend *Tao Teh Ching*, and other ancient Chinese texts, requires the reader to think complementarily and to understand rationally and to innerstand transrationally. *Tao Teh Ching* is not written in a linear manner, like most treatises in Western philosophy, that is, one chapter logically building upon the argument made in the previous chapter. Each of the eighty-one passages of *Tao Teh Ching* holographically contains the whole of *Tao Teh Ching*.

Transrational *innerstanding* arises when the reader contemplates into the *whole* of a passage as well as of the text *vertically*, whereas rational *understanding* arises when the reader contemplates upon the *totality* of the text *horizontally*. Wholeness is indivisible, while totality is divisible. Through the contemplation upon the totality of the text, rational understanding comes as the symbolic representations and the conceptual distinctions of the Tao. Through the contemplation into the wholeness within the passage and the entire text, transrational innerstanding comes as the direct experience of the Tao and the experiential knowing of the undefinable. Together these two modes of knowing complementarily benefit our balanced, integral spiritual and intellectual development.

2. TEH

The Chinese word *teh* (in Japanese *toku*) is variously translated in English as *virtue, power,* or *integrity,* none of which really captures its full meaning. The Chinese character *teh* consists of three subcharacters, which individually mean (1) "to go around"; (2) "to inspect"; and (3) "the heart (of awareness)." *Teh* originally depicted the action of the government sending high officials to provinces around the country for inspection. As a result of such inspection, a provincial political order was developed and maintained. Hence the power of inspection was order-generating, which was understood to be the power of consciousness, and thus the third subcharacter, the heart of awareness, was added to complete the formation of the character and the meaning matrix of *teh*.

Therefore, *teh* signifies the order-generating awareness and the order generated by such awareness. *Teh* is the *self-originating virtue* based not on outer codes of morality but on inner self-awareness and in-depth inspection of oneself and the world that engenders order within and without. When *teh* is wholly in accord with the Tao, it becomes *Tao Teh,* the Virtue of the Tao. *Tao Teh Ching* is the book on the Kosmic Virtue of the Tao (ethics) as well as on the Tao itself (metaphysics).

In this translation, *teh* is usually translated as virtue in the above meaning. However, depending on a context, the meaning of the English term "virtue," as the term "teh" in the original Chinese, may mean more traditional virtue that is based more on external moral codes than inner awareness. For instance, in the thirty-eighth passage, the *teh* in the sense of self-originating virtue is designated by the term "authentic virtue," while the *teh* in the more traditional sense is designated by the term "inauthentic virtue."

3. CHING

Ching designates a sacred classic in the Chinese canon. Of the three canonical Taoist texts, *I Ching* has sixty-four parts, while *Tao Teh Ching* and *T'ai Hsuan Ching* have eighty-one parts. The ancient Chinese Taoist sages intuitively knew that there were two sets of logic operative in the universe: binary (*yin-yang*) logic and ternary (*t'ien-ti-jen*) logic. They further knew that the binary logic is primarily operative in the physical-phenomenal universe, the universe of effect, while the ternary logic is operative in the spiritual-noumenal universe, the universe of cause, inclusive of the physical-phenomenal universe.

I Ching is primarily a book of life in the visible and phenomenal plane, and therefore is based on the binary logic of *yin* and *yang* with the ternary logic as its substratum. Hence, it is expressed in the combinations of hexagram, a mathematical diagram consisting of six lines, each line being either solid (*yang*-positive) or broken (*yin*-negative). There are sixty-four (2^6 or $2^3 \times 2^3$) possible arrangements of these two types of lines. Thus, *I Ching* consists of sixty-four parts, which are sixty-four facets of life lessons of this world.

Tao Teh Ching is a book of life both in the invisible, noumenal, spiritual plane and in the visible, phenomenal, material plane, and therefore is based on the ternary logic of *t'ien, ti,* and *jen* with the binary logic as its substratum. Hence, it is expressed in the combinations of tetragram, a mathematical diagram consisting of four stacked lines of three types—solid (*t'ien*-positive), broken (*ti*-negative), and twice-broken (*jen*-indeterminate/free-will element). There are eighty-one (3^4 or $3^2 \times 3^2$) possible arrangement of these three types of lines. Thus, *Tao Teh Ching* consists of eighty-one parts, which are eighty-one facets of life lessons of both this (visible-phenomenal) and the other (invisible-noumenal) worlds.

T'ai Hsuan Ching, The Book of Great Invisible, is primarily a book of life in the invisible, noumenal, spiritual plane, and therefore is based on the ternary logic as *Tao Teh Ching* and is likewise expressed in the combinations of tetragram and in eighty-one parts. To study Taoism in its totality, this translator suggests that the reader study all three of these canonical Taoist texts.

The reader may read *Tao Teh Ching* randomly, instead of linearly from one passage to the next. The reader may also use tetragram for reading *Tao Teh Ching*, just as people use hexagram in the form of divination for reading *I Ching*. No matter in what order one reads it, *Tao Teh Ching* can remain a continual source of perennial wisdom for the rest of one's life. As the eighty-one passages of the book contain the great sage's lifetime of wisdom, it is worthy of a lifetime of study.

4. TRANSLATION

This translation is unique in the following ways:

1. The whole text has been translated based on the translator's sound knowledge in the esoteric Taoist science and philosophy.

2. The translator consulted the latest etymological study of ancient Chinese words done by the foremost Japanese scholar and recognized authority of the Chinese language, Professor Shizuka Shirakawa, which contains a considerable amount of new findings, shedding light on the deeper etymological meanings of key concepts throughout the text.

3. The original Chinese text available to us today does not appear to be the work of a single author. It is this translator's understanding as well as the opinion of many reputable scholars that following the writing of the original, several Taoists subsequently added their commentary to the text, which was passed on as the official text attributed to Lao Tzu, the legendary Taoist

Master, a contemporary of Confucius, who is the likely author of the original.

This translator translated these inserted comments *in the context of* the original so that each passage is coherently structured, conveying a coherent meaning. When we read many of the other translations, as fine as they are as translations, we encounter paragraphs that do not fit into the whole passages in which they appear. In this translation, such incoherence in text has been minimized or eliminated without changing textual meaning.

4. Translation is not the one-for-one transposition of words but the re-creation in another language of the whole matrix of meaning that is the original text. Especially between two languages as different as Chinese and English, no metaphrase or word-for-word transposition-*qua*-translation is possible. Therefore, this translation is definitely a paraphrase in English of the original Chinese text.

5. This translator reads ancient Chinese in the form of Kanbun, which is the ancient Japanese way of reading Chinese. Each Chinese character has a set of meanings. Therefore, the learned reader can comprehend Chinese texts, if he or she knows meanings of words, without knowing how the words are pronounced in Chinese in its various dialects. While lack of knowledge of Chinese proper may be a certain disadvantage, the knowledge of Kanbun and of Japanese has given this translator the advantage of benefiting from the scholarship of both Chinese and Japanese scholars, which is reflected in this translation.

It is my sincere wish and my reason for translating *Tao Teh Ching* that the reader of *The Book of Balance* may find not only enjoyment and insight but also inspiration for his or her own spiritual and character development, as I have found through reading the original.

— Yasuhiko Genku Kimura

THE BOOK OF BALANCE

LAO TZU'S *TAO TEH CHING*

ONE

The Tao Eternal is beyond definition.
No name given can capture its eternality.

Nameless, it is the origin of the Kosmos.
Named, it is the beginning of all things.

Nothingness, it is the inner being of the Kosmos.
Thingness, it is the outer distinctions of the Kosmos.

These two, though different in names,
      arise from the same source:
The source called the Invisible.

Invisible beyond the invisible,
It is the entry into the myriad wonders
      of the Eternal Kosmos.

道可道章第一

Two

When the world recognizes beauty as beauty, ugliness arises.
When the world recognizes good as good, evil arises.

Being and non-being create each other.
Difficult and easy define each other.
Long and short form each other.
High and low support each other.
Tone and voice accompany each other.
Before and after follow each other.

Hence, the sage lives in the state of non-action—
        of eternal balance,
And teaches by the precept of silence—
        and through his silent deed.
He accepts things as they arise,
Creates without possessing,
Performs without depending,
Accomplishes without claiming credit.

Because he does not claim credit for himself,
His virtues endure forever more.

天下皆知章第二

24

THREE

When the learned is not over esteemed,
There will not be unnecessary competition
        amongst people.
When the treasure is not over valued,
There will not be acts of stealing amongst people.
When we do not show people things
        that stir up their wants,
Their minds will not be disturbed.

Therefore, the sage governs the people by
Restoring balance in value and worth, through
Emptying people's minds and filling their essence,
Weakening their ambition and strengthening their character,
Freeing them from knowledge and wants, and
Keeping the learned from over exercising their authority.

Act in accordance with the principle of non-action—
        of eternal balance,
Then order will arise of itself.

FOUR

Empty of all doctrines,
The Tao is wisdom eternally inexhaustible.
Fathomless for the mere intellect,
The Tao is the law wherewith all things come into being.

It blunts the edges of the intellect,
Untangles the knots of the mind,
Softens the glare of thinking,
And settles the dust of thought.

Transparent yet invisible,
The Tao exists like deep pellucid water.
Its origin is unknown,
For it existed before Heaven and Earth.

道沖章第四

FIVE

The Kosmos is not humane;
Impartially, it treats all things as transitory.
The sage is not humane;
Impartially, he treats all people as transitory.
Manifesting the Tao Eternal,
The kosmic space is like a bellows.
Empty, yet inexhaustible,
The more one activates it, the more it generates.

Being full, too many words lead one nowhere;
Impartially, keep to the silent core of emptiness.

天地不仁章第五

Six

The Tao, the Spirit of the Valley, is immortal.
It is called the Primordial Female.

The Gate of the Primordial Female,
Through its opening and closing,
Performs the kosmic intercourse,
And is called the origin of Heaven and Earth,

Eternally existing,
Forever tireless.

SEVEN

Heaven is eternal and earth everlasting.
They thus endure forever,
Because they exist not for themselves
But for the whole, selflessly.

Whereby the sage,
Existing selflessly for the whole,
Puts himself behind and thereby finds himself foremost,
Holds himself outside and thereby finds himself inmost.

He has no self apart from the whole,
Wherefore he realizes the self that is the whole.

EIGHT

The highest good is like water,
Benefiting all but contending with none,
Flowing in low places which the masses disdain.
Hence, it is close to the goodness of the Tao.

In dwelling, be grounded,
In thinking, be deep,
In giving, be balanced,
In speaking, be truthful,
In governing, be orderly,
In working, be competent,
In action, be timely.

In following the virtues of water,
The sage contends with no one,
And therefore he invites no troubles in life.

NINE

To fill to the brim is to be out of balance,
Wherefore it is better to stop before overfilling.

To over-sharpen a sword is to be out of balance,
Wherefore its edge will not last long.

To line a hall with gold and jade is to be out of balance,
Wherefore no one can guard them.

If wealth and rank make a man haughty and clinging,
He will surely bequeath misfortune upon himself.

If success is achieved and honor bestowed,
Quietly withdraw from your position.

This is the Way of Heaven.

TEN

In accordance with the Tao Eternal,

Embrace your body and mind in oneness
        without any diremption.
Enliven your vital energy
        until it reaches the suppleness of a baby.
Cleanse your mind to eliminate all unclarity.
Love your people and lead your community
        without unbalanced action.
Be receptive as a gentle female
        in the rhythmic intercourse of the Kosmos.
Remain in the state of not-knowing
        while achieving knowledge in all fields.

This is the spiritual virtue of the Kosmos:
Birthing life without possessing,
Nurturing life without expecting,
Rearing life without dominating.

ELEVEN

Thirty spokes share a hub;
The usefulness of the cart
      lies in the space where there is nothing.

Clay is kneaded into a vessel;
The usefulness of the vessel
      lies in the space where there is nothing.

A room is created by cutting out doors and windows;
The usefulness of the room
      lies in the space where there is nothing.

Therefore,
The benefit of things lies in the usefulness of nothing.

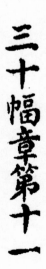

TWELVE

The five colors blind the inner eye.
The five tones deafen the inner ear.
The five flavors dull the inner tongue.

In pursuit of outer pleasures,
Racing and hunting madden the inner mind,
Rare goods obstruct inner progress.

Therefore,
The sage attends to that which is within,
      not that which is without.
He lives from the center, not from the periphery.

THIRTEEN

Honor and disgrace both startle people.
Undue significance is attached to such tribulations
        as though they were matters of life and death.

Honor and disgrace both startle people,
Because honor means higher and disgrace means lower
        in the opinion of others.
Hence, they become startled with pleasure
        when honor is given,
And they become startled with displeasure
        when honor is taken away.

Undue significance is attached to such tribulations
        as though they were matters of life and death,
For people think the physical self is real.
If people realize the unreality of the physical self,
How can they attach significance to such tribulations
        as honor or disgrace?

Therefore, only one who values the world as oneself
        is fit to tend the world;
Only one who loves the world as oneself
        can be entrusted with the care of the world.

FOURTEEN

Looked at but not seen, it is thus called the invisible,
Listened to but not heard, it is thus called the inaudible,
Reached for but not grasped, it is thus called the intangible:

These three are beyond the reach of sense and reason,
Yet, in the moment of kosmic union,
They merge in spiritual awareness as the Universal One.

There is no above that is bright, nor below that is dark,
But only the infinite, forever indefinable,
        always reverting to nothingness.
Therefore, it is called form of the formless,
        image of the imageless.
And it is known as the amorphous.

Confronting it, no head is seen from the front.
Following it, no rear is seen from behind.

Whereby one lives in the present
        in accordance with the Tao Eternal,
Thereby one comes to know the beginning of time.

This is called the Universal Law of the Tao.

視之不見章第十四

FIFTEEN

The embodiment of the Tao Eternal,
The ancient masters are wondrously subtle
        and profoundly penetrating.
The depth of their being is unfathomable
        and beyond comprehension.

As their depth is unfathomable and beyond comprehension,
Only their appearance can be incompletely described:

The master is as alert as a person fording a winter stream,
As careful as a person watchful of his surroundings,
As respectful as a thoughtful guest,
As flowing as melting ice,
As plain as an unhewn log,
As empty as an open valley,
As inclusive as turbid waters.

Who could keep still until turbid waters
        become clear of their own accord?
Who could stay calm until still waters
        become alive of their own accord?

Those who embody the Tao do not desire
        to extend themselves to the fullest.
For, the Tao is balance,
        and there is no fullest, no extreme.
Therefore, through balance, they refill their essence
        and renew their life force forevermore.

古之善為士章第十五

SIXTEEN

Attain utmost emptiness,
Maintain utter stillness.

Then, as ten thousand things arise together,
One will witness their returning to the source.

Though things abound in the universe,
They all return to the source.

Returning to the source is called stillness,
And stillness is called returning to destiny.

To return to destiny is to return to eternity,
And to know eternity is called enlightenment.

To act unawarely in the nescience of eternity
Is to bring disaster to your life.

To know eternity is to be all-inclusive,
To be all-inclusive is to be impartial,
To be impartial is to attain self-mastery,
To attain self-mastery is to be Heavenly,
And to be Heavenly is to be one with the Tao Eternal.

To be one with the Tao Eternal
            is to enjoy everlasting life,
Forever secure
            even after the enfolding of the physical self.

SEVENTEEN

The supreme leader is one whose existence is barely known.

Next best is one who is loved and praised.

Next is one who is feared.

The last is one who is contemned.

No trust will ever be accorded
        to a leader who lacks integrity.

Therefore, with deep commitment,
Honor your words and trust the words of others.

Then, when the work is done and success achieved,
The people will say, "We did it ourselves."

EIGHTEEN

When the inner truth of the Tao is lost,
The outer code of morality comes into being.

When cleverness reigns in the world,
Hypocrisy becomes rampant;

When discord arises in the family,
Filiality is emphasized;

When chaos befalls the nation,
Respect is accorded to loyal subjects alone.

NINETEEN

Abandon the relative notions of holiness and wisdom,
And people will benefit a hundred-fold.

Abandon the outer codes of benevolence and rectitude,
And people will return to natural filiality and kindness;

Abandon the unbalanced acts of cleverness and profiteering,
And there will be no robbers or thieves.

By looking within,

Evince the inner self,
Embrace the unadorned truth;

Diminish the outer self,
Demolish the phantasmic desire.

Abandon the external search for knowledge,
Abolish the internal worry for illusory matters.

TWENTY

To cease unnecessary learning
      is to be free from unnecessary concerns.
How much difference is there between yes and no?
How much distinction is there between good and bad?
Must one fear what everyone fears
      or value what everyone values?
In all this, there is no universality,
      and thus no end to confusion.

Jolly are the masses in chasing after excitement,
As though feasting at a royal feast, or
Ascending a high tower on a spring day.

Quiet am I by abiding in the stillness of being,
Like a newborn babe as yet to even smile,
Being here and now, and having nowhere to go.

The masses all hoard more than they need.
Forgetful of possessing, I alone am bereft.

My mind is like that of a fool, for I know nothing.
The ordinary man is bright, while I alone seem dark.
The ordinary man is clear, while I alone seem muddled.
Without boundary, I am like the vast ocean,
Without restriction, I am like a gentle wind.

The masses all have things to do;
I alone remain stubbornly unoccupied.

Thus, I am uniquely different from the rest,
Honoring the Tao from which I take my sustenance.

42

TWENTY-ONE

The outer expression of great virtue
         follows the inner subtlety of the Tao.
Yet, the inner subtlety of the Tao
         is altogether elusive and ineffable.

Elusive and ineffable, yet there arises some image within;
Ineffable and elusive, yet there exists some thing within;
Cavernous and dark, yet there is some essence within;
This essence is entirely real; in it is Kosmic Integrity.

Hitherto, the name of Kosmic Integrity has endured,
And remains the Principle
         of Kosmic Creation and Decreation.

By what means do I know the Principle
         of Kosmic Creation and Decreation?
By means of Kosmic Integrity itself.

Twenty-two

To yield is to prevail;
To bend is to straighten;
To be hollow is to be full;
To die is to regenerate.

To have little is to receive much;
To have much is to be confused.

Wherefore,
The sage embraces the complementary oneness of existence,
And sets an exemplary pattern for the rest of the world.

He does not display his ability,
Therefore his being shines forth.
He is not self-righteous,
Therefore he becomes distinguished.
He does not take credit,
Therefore he becomes recognized.
He is not self-important,
Therefore he is made a leader.
He does not contend with the world,
Therefore the world does not contend with him.

The old admonition that "to yield is to prevail"
            is not an empty adage.
Truly, to yield is to prevail, and in prevailing,
            one returns to oneness.

曲則全章第二十二

TWENTY-THREE

To be silent is natural, for silence alone endures in Nature.

A whirlwind does not last the whole morning;
Nor does a downpour last the whole day.
Nature cannot make her commotion last;
Nor can human beings make their commotion last.

Therefore, in enduring silence, without commotion,
The master creates harmony with all humanity,

Sharing the experience of the Tao
        with those who embody the Tao;
Sharing the experience of virtue
        with those who practice virtue;
Sharing the experience of loss
        with those who lose virtue.

Thereby, in sharing the experience,

Those who embody the Tao enjoy his company;
Those who practice virtue enjoy his company;
Those who lose virtue enjoy his company.

The master is silent, for he knows the Tao
        and trusts the universe.

Therefore, be silent, then you will be enduring;
Trust, then you will be trusted.

希言自然章第二十三

TWENTY-FOUR

A man who tiptoes cannot stand.
A man who straddles cannot walk.
A man who flaunts himself cannot shine.

A man who is self-righteous is not respected.
A man who is self-boasting is not acknowledged.
A man who is self-conceited is not promoted.

From the viewpoint of the Tao,
These behaviors are like excess food and excrescent flesh.

Creation abhors such imbalance,
And thus the man of the Tao does not abide in them.

跂者不立章第二十四

TWENTY-FIVE

Before the birth of Heaven and Earth is Being,
          formless yet complete.

Silent and still,
All one and unchanging, all present and unending,
It may be regarded as the Matrix of the Universe.
Its true name is unknown,
So we call it by its alias, the Tao,
And name it by its designation, the Great.

Being great, it extends without limit,
Extending without limit, it is far-reaching,
Being far-reaching, it returns to itself.

The Tao is great,
Heaven is great,
Earth is great,
And Man is also great.

These are the four greatnesses of the Kosmos,
And of them Man is one.
Man patterns after Earth,
Earth patterns after Heaven,
Heaven patterns after the Tao,
And the Tao patterns after that which is natural.

有物混成章第二十五

Twenty-six

Heaviness is the center of lightness.
Stillness is the master of commotion.

For this reason,
The sage may travel the whole day,
Yet stays centered, without leaving his heavy baggage cart.
Or he may enjoy a splendid view,
Yet stays serene, calmly transcending all outward pleasures.

Why should the lord of ten thousand chariots
        behave lightly before all under Heaven?

One who behaves lightly loses one's center.
One who behaves agitatedly loses one's mastery.

重為輕根章第二十六

Twenty-seven

The master in his action is so complete
    that he leaves no trace behind.
The master in his conversation is so balanced
    that he leaves no discord behind.

The master in his thinking is so original
That he depends on no external authority.

The master in protecting people is so skillful
That, without any visible means, he renders
    all attempts for invasion ineffectual.

The master in uniting people is so adept
    That, without any visible means, he renders
        all efforts for disunity ineffectual.

Thus, the master, without abandoning anyone,
    is always good at empowering people

And, without abandoning anything,
    is always good at utilizing things.

This is the all-embracing wisdom of the Tao.
Hence, the virtuous is the teacher of the non-virtuous,
While the non-virtuous serves as
    the lessons for the virtuous.

If you value not your teacher or cherish not your lessons,
No matter how intelligent and informed you are,
    you are greatly deluded.

This is the essential, subtle truth of the Tao.

善行無轍迹章第二十七

49

TWENTY-EIGHT

Knowing the strength of the masculine principle,
Yet remaining in the lovingness of feminine virtue,
One becomes the stream of life to which other streams conjoin.

In thus becoming the stream of life for the world,
One comes to embody perennial virtue,
And returns to pristine innocence.

Knowing the purity of kosmic harmony,
Yet remaining in the impurity of worldly discord,
One becomes the standard of life by which other people can live.

In thus becoming the standard of life for the world,
One comes to reaffirm perennial virtue,
And returns to inner infinity.

Knowing the glory of public acclaim,
Yet remaining in the obscurity of personal humility,
One becomes the valley of life
      in which other people can repose.
In thus becoming the valley of life for the world,
One comes to fulfill perennial virtue,
And returns to undivided simplicity.
Undivided simplicity is reduced
      to mere usefulness through division.
Remaining undivided,
      the sage makes masterful use of the divided,
And is made the leader of an organization.

Thus, the great organization led by a sage
      is undivided and whole.

TWENTY-NINE

Those who want to take control of the world by force
        can never succeed,
For the world is a sacred vessel of dynamic energy,
        not meant to be controlled.

Those who try to forcibly control it will ruin it.
Those who try to forcibly keep it will lose it.

Because life is not a static entity but a dynamic process,
Sometimes one moves ahead and sometimes follows behind.
Sometimes one works hard and sometimes takes rest.
Sometimes one grows strong and sometimes grows weak.
Sometimes one is supported and sometimes is unsupported.

Wherefore, the sage,
        knowingly moving with the dynamic flow of life,
Avoids extremes, avoids extravagance, and avoids excess.

将欲取天下章第二十九

THIRTY

Those who assist national leaders by means of the Tao,
Never use military force to make their nations world powers.

No action is ever without a repercussion:

Wherever an army is stationed,
        there grow briars and brambles.
Wherever a battle is fought, there follows a famine.

A good general in the direst necessity of a war
Achieves his purpose of winning the war,
But never seeks to gain power over others.

Therefore, achieve your purpose, but only if it is called for;
Achieve your purpose, but never be haughty;
Achieve your purpose, but never be boastful;
Achieve your purpose, but never be supercilious;
Achieve your purpose, but never be overpowering.

Whenever something reaches an extreme in strength,
        it will inevitably decline.

This is called the way against the Tao.
The way against the Tao always leads to an early demise.

以道佐人章第三十

THIRTY-ONE

Weapons are instruments of ill omen;
        all creatures abhor them.
Therefore, the man of the Tao never abides in them.

The virtuous man usually honors the left, the positive,
But, when called to be in a battlefield,
        honors the right, the negative.

Weapons are instruments of ill omen,
Not instruments of the virtuous man.

Therefore, when he is compelled to resort to them,
He uses them with utmost restraint and calmness.

He does not glorify victory, for glorifying victory means
        to take delight in killing.
And whosoever takes delight in killing
        will never find success in this world.

On occasions for celebration,
        the positive left is given priority,
On occasions for mourning,
        the negative right is given priority.
The lieutenant stands on the left,
        and the general on the right.
That is, they stand in accordance
        with mourning ritual.

The killing of masses of human beings
        we bewail with deep sorrow and grief.
The victory in battle we observe with rites of mourning.

THIRTY-TWO

The Tao remains eternally unnamable.

As undivided simplicity,
If it resides in an ordinary person,
        nobody in the world can subjugate him;
If an influential person abides by it,
        everybody in the world will be drawn to him.

When heaven and earth come together in harmony,
Showering the world equally
        with the sweet rain of undivided simplicity,
People cooperate voluntarily without any governing rules.

When simplicity is divided, names come into existence.
When names are already there,
        the process of further division should stop,
For to know when to stop
        is to avoid the danger of complexity.

The Tao is to the world
        what the ocean is to the rivers of the earth.

THIRTY-THREE

To know others is wisdom;
To know one's self is enlightenment.

To conquer others is power;
To conquer one's self is strength.

One who knows what is enough is wealthy;
One who does what is required is committed.

One who stays in one's destiny endures;
One who dies without perishing lives forever.

知人者章第三十三

THIRTY-FOUR

The Great Tao overflows everywhere in the universe.
It suffuses with life all beings
      that depend on it for their existence.

It accomplishes everything while remaining nameless.
It nurtures everything while claiming no mastership.

It desires nothing for itself,
      and is therefore called the Small.
It is the source whereto everything returns,
      and is therefore called the Vast.

Thus, the sage never thinks
      of claiming greatness for himself,
Yet, for this very reason, achieves true greatness.

大道汎兮章第三十四

Thirty-Five

From the great formless imagining
       the world emerges into existence,
Without obstruction,
       but with balance, harmony, and peace.

Music and feast provide fleeting pleasures
       in this ephemeral world.
The Tao in its utterance
       brings no such pleasures to the senses.

The Tao, when looked at, cannot be seen by the eye.
The Tao, when listened to, cannot be heard by the ear.

Yet, when used, it is forever inexhaustible.

THIRTY-SIX

What is ultimately to be compressed
        must first be expanded.
What is ultimately to be weakened
        must first be strengthened.
What is ultimately to be discarded
        must first be promoted.
What is ultimately to be taken away must first be given.

This is the subtle light of wisdom.

The soft overcomes the hard.
The weak overcomes the strong.

The fish should never leave the water.
The formed should never leave the formless.

THIRTY-SEVEN

The Tao does nothing,
Yet it leaves nothing undone.

If the leaders of the world abide by it,
All beings of their own accord will transform themselves.

If in the course of self-transformation
        discordant desires arise,
Calm them with the unnameable simplicity of the Tao.

If calmed with the nameless simplicity of the Tao,
Discordant desires of their own accord will disappear.

If discordant desires disappear and quietude is restored,
The world of its own accord will order itself.

道常無為章第三十七

Thirty-eight

The person of authentic virtue makes no issue of his virtue.
Therefore, he is virtuous, wholly and completely.
The person of inauthentic virtue makes much issue of his virtue.
Therefore, he is not virtuous, wholly and completely.

Authentic virtue is a matter of being, not of doing.
Therefore, the person of authentic virtue
        makes no claims for his virtuous action.
Inauthentic virtue is a matter of doing, not of being.
Therefore, the person of inauthentic virtue
        makes claims for his virtuous action.

Superior benevolence is a matter of doing.
Yet the person of superior benevolence
        makes no claims for his benevolent deeds.
Superior rectitude is a matter of doing.
And the person of superior rectitude
        makes claims for his righteous deeds.

Superior etiquette is a matter of doing.
But the person of superior etiquette,
If people do not conform to his standard,
Will pull their elbows and force them to conform.

When the Tao is lost, then comes virtue.
When virtue is lost, then comes benevolence.
When benevolence is lost, then comes rectitude.
When rectitude is lost, then comes etiquette.

Etiquette is but the attenuation of probity
      and the beginning of disorder.
Prescience is but a flower of the Tao
      and the beginning of nescience.

For this reason,
The person of character dwells in the depths within,
      not in the shallows without.
He dwells in the fruitful substance within,
      not in the flowery embellishment without.
He thus chooses the inner and discards the outer.

THIRTY-NINE

In ancient times, these attained wholeness:

Heaven attained wholeness and thereby became pure.
Earth attained wholeness and thereby became tranquil.
Spirits attained wholeness and thereby became divine.
Valleys attained wholeness and thereby became full.
Beings attained wholeness and thereby became alive.
Leaders attained wholeness and thereby all was put aright.

Everything is what it is by virtue of its wholeness.

Heaven without purity would rend.
Earth without tranquility would collapse.
Spirits without divinity would dissipate.
Valleys without fullness would desiccate.
Beings without aliveness would perish.
Leaders without magnanimity would fall.

Humility is the basis of magnanimity.
Modesty is the fundament of exaltation.

Those in high position call themselves
      powerless, unworthy, or destitute.
Is this not because they take humility
      as the basis of magnanimity?

There is no honor in displaying your honor.
Desire not either to be jingling like jade
      or to be stolid like stone.

昔之得一章第三十九

FORTY

Cyclic returning to the source
      is the rhythmic movement of the Tao.
Gentle spontaneity is the nature of its function.

All beings derive their beingness from Being,
      which is the Tao.
And Being arises in and as Nothingness, which is the Tao.

FORTY-ONE

When a superior person hears the Tao,
He practices it committedly.
When a mediocre person hears the Tao,
He practices it sometimes,
        but just as often ignores it.
When an inferior person hears the Tao,
He roars with disparaging laughter.
If he did not laugh, it would not be the Tao.

Thus the age-old epigrams state:

The enlightening way appears dark.
The advancing way appears retreating.
The level way appears bumpy.
The highest virtue appears ordinary.
The purest goodness appears sullied.
The abundant virtue appears deficient.
The perfect virtue appears defective.
The most genuine appears insincere.
The greatest space has no corners.
The greatest talent ripens late.
The greatest voice is silent.
The greatest image is formless.

The Tao is hidden and has no name.
Yet the Tao alone bestows the power
        and fulfills the destiny of everything.

上士聞道章第四十一

FORTY-TWO

The Tao, the wholeness, gives rise to oneness.
Oneness gives rise to complementary unity.
Complementary unity gives rise
      to complementary trinity.
Complementary trinity gives rise
      to everything in existence.
Everything consists of the complementarity
      of *yang* in the center and *yin* surrounding it.
From the balanced interchange between the two
      arises equilibrium in disequilibrium.

Ordinary people hate nothing more
      than to be powerless, unworthy, or destitute.
Yet this is what people in high position call themselves.
This means, in accordance with
      the principle of complementarity,
That to lose is to gain and to gain is to lose.

Let me repeat what others have taught:
The strong and violent, being out of balance,
      do not die natural deaths.
This is the very foundation of my teaching.

FORTY-THREE

The softest under heaven always prevails over the hardest.
For, having no fixed form,
It can penetrate even where there is no visible opening.

This is the power of balanced action through nonaction.
This is the benefit of balanced action through nonaction.

Nonaction teaches without words,
        and benefits without actions.
No power in the world can even come close to it.

天下之至柔章第四十三

FORTY-FOUR

Which is more precious, fame or health?
Which is more important, health or wealth?
Which is more painful, gaining or losing?

The more excessive is your attachment,
The greater is your suffering.

The more excessive is your possession,
The heavier is your loss.

To know what is enough is to be free from disgrace.
To know when to stop is to be free from danger.

Those who practice this will long endure.

FORTY-FIVE

Great perfection appears imperfect,
Yet there is no end to its process of perfecting.

Great fullness appears empty,
Yet there is no limit to its process of fulfilling.

Great uprightness appears bent,
Great mastery seems clumsy,
Great eloquence sounds awkward,
Yet they keep growing without limitations.

Movement overcomes stagnation.
Stillness overcomes discordance.

Movement and stillness in balance
Set the world in evolutionary order.

大成若缺章第四十五

FORTY-SIX

When the world follows the Tao,
Horses are used to fertilize the farm fields.
When the world does not follow the Tao,
Even mares are expended to breed in the battlefields.

When the individual follows the Tao,
Energy is used in his harmonious inner development.
When the individual does not follow the Tao,
Energy is expended in his continuous inner conflict.

There is no greater vice than giving in to greed,
No greater calamity than not knowing contentment,
No greater imputation than succumbing to covetousness.

Therefore, know and be content with what is enough,
Then you will always have enough.

天下有道章第四十六

FORTY-SEVEN

Without going out the door,
You can know the ways of the world.

Without looking out the window,
You can know the ways of heaven.

The farther you go outward, the less you know.

Thus, the sage knows without going outward,
Understands without looking outward,
Accomplishes without acting outward.

不出戶章第四十七

FORTY-EIGHT

The practice of ordinary learning increases complexity daily.
The practice of the Tao increases simplicity daily.

Simplicity leads to more simplicity,
Until it reaches the state of pristine nonaction.

Then nothing is done, yet nothing remains undone.

Thus, one who wins the world does so
By not meddling with it, through nonaction, with simplicity.

One who loses the world does so
By meddling with it, through action, with complexity.

FORTY-NINE

The sage does not have a set mind.
His mind is unconditioned, and
He regards the minds of all people as his own.

He is good to those who are good.
He is good to those who are not good.
For his virtue is goodness itself.

He is in integrity with those of integrity.
He is in integrity with those without integrity.
For his virtue is integrity itself.

The sage, to serve this world,
In compassion merges his mind with all minds.

People rivet their eyes and ears
        upon differences amongst them.
The sage, with childlike innocence,
        sees one humanity in all.

聖人無常心章第四十九

FIFTY

Life is appearance; death is disappearance.

Three out of ten live a long life.
Three out of ten live a short life.
Three out of ten bring upon themselves an untimely death,
Because they cling too much to outer pleasures of life.

He who maintains a balanced life in accordance with the Tao,
Does not meet tigers or rhinoceroses in the wilderness,
Does not suffer attacks from the enemy in the battlefield.

Upon him the tiger has no place to fasten its claws,
The rhinoceros has no place to jab its horn,
The weapon has no place to pierce its blade.

Why is this so?
Because in him there is no room for death to enter.

出生入死章第五十

FIFTY-ONE

The Tao begets existence.
Intelligence nurtures existence.
Substance forms existence.
Forces complete existence.

For this reason,
Everything in existence, without exception,
Reveres the Tao and honors Intelligence,
Not by any decree, but with utter spontaneity.

Thus, the Tao begets everything in existence,
And Intelligence nurtures it,
          Rears it,
          Develops it,
          Completes it,
          Ripens it,
          Sustains it,
          Protects it.

Giving birth without possessing,
Availing life without claiming,
Promoting growth without controlling,
These are the Profound Virtues of Kosmic Intelligence.

FIFTY-TWO

The universe has an origin, the Matrix of Creation,
Functioning as the Mother of the world.

If you know the Mother, you will know her children.
If you know her children while abiding with the Mother,
Though your body may be dissolved,
Your life-energy will remain inexhaustible.

Close the cracks, close the doors of the senses,
Then, till the end of your life
        you will not be drained of energy.
Open the cracks and react to external stimulations,
Then, till the end of your life
        you will not be saved from suffering.

To perceive the subtle is enlightenment.
To abide in gentleness is strength.
Use your inner light to return to enlightenment
And you will not inherit any harm.

This is called "learning the eternal lesson."

天下有始章第五十二

FIFTY-THREE

With clear, appreciative discernment,
I choose to walk the great way of the Tao,
And fear naught save going astray.

The great way is very smooth and straight,
Yet people prefer uneven and winding by-paths, and thus go astray.
Therefore, in the world that has gone astray,
While the courts are clean and decorated,
The fields are untilled and the granaries are empty.

If the ruler wears fancy clothes,
Carries around sharp swords,
Indulges in extravagant food and drink,
And possesses more riches than he needs,
He is indeed a brazen bandit.

This is contrary to the great way of the Tao.

FIFTY-FOUR

What is firmly established within cannot be uprooted.
What is firmly embraced within cannot be disengaged.
The Tao, thus firmly established and embraced within you,
Will be respected for generations to come.

Cultivate the Tao in your character,
Then its virtues will be genuine.
Cultivate the Tao in your family,
Then its virtues will abound.
Cultivate the Tao in your community,
Then its virtues will endure.
Cultivate the Tao in your country,
Then its virtues will flourish.
Cultivate the Tao in the world,
Then its virtues will pervade.

Therefore, you can observe the virtues of the Tao,
In your character,
        if you cultivate it in your character;
In your family,
        if you cultivate it in your family;
In your community,
        if you cultivate it in your community;
In your country,
        if you cultivate it in your country;
And in the world,
        if you cultivate it in the world.

How can you know how the state of the world is?
Simply by thus observing.

善建不拔章第五十四

FIFTY-FIVE

He who embodies the fullness of the Tao is like a ruddy infant.

No poisonous wasps will sting him.
No fierce beasts will seize him.
No rapacious birds will maul him.
His bones are tender and muscles soft,
Yet his grip is tight.
He knows not of the union of male and female,
Yet, filled with vitality,
His manhood becomes vigorously erect.
He can howl all day without becoming hoarse,
Because he is the embodiment of perfect balance.

To know balance is to know the eternal.
To know the eternal is to be illumined.

To overprotect life is to invite sure disaster.
To overuse the mind is to invite lopsided strength.
To overdevelop a thing is to invite early decay.

All are out of balance, and thus contrary to the Tao.
Being contrary to the Tao, things soon cease to be.

FIFTY-SIX

Those who know do not talk.
Those who talk do not know.

Close the openings of your senses,
Blunt the sharpness of your intellect,
Untie the tangles of your attachment,
Soften the brightness of your knowledge.

Be one with the dust of the world.
This is to be one with the Tao.

He who is one with the Tao
        cannot be courted,
        cannot be distanced,
        cannot be bought,
        cannot be harmed,
        cannot be honored,
        cannot be humiliated.

For this reason, he becomes the true treasure of the world.

知者不言章第五十六

Fifty-Seven

Govern a nation with enduring justice.
Command troops with unpredictable moves.
Lead the world with empowering noninterference.

How do I know this to be so?
From witnessing the following:

The more restrictions there are in the world,
      the poorer people become.
The more weapons people possess,
      the darker nations become.
The more cunning and cleverness there is,
      the more there are anomalous things.
The more rules and regulations there are,
      the more there are thieves and robbers.

Therefore the sage says:

I take no action,
      and people are naturally transformed.
I delight in stillness,
      and people naturally do what is right.
I do not interfere,
      and people on their own prosper.
I have no greed,
      and people on their own return to simplicity.

以正治國章第五十七

FIFTY-EIGHT

When the government
        is inwardly contained and disciplined,
The people become wholesome and good.
When the government
        is outwardly demanding and exacting,
The people become tense and cunning.

Fortune rests on misfortune.
Misfortune hides in fortune.
There is no end to their perpetual cyclic interchange.

Likewise, there is nothing that is permanently fitting.
What is fitting eventually becomes unfitting.
What is proper eventually becomes improper.

Not knowing the complementarity
        inherent in cyclic interchange,
People's delusion of permanence
        tends to last for a long time.

Thus, knowing the dynamic balance
        existing in complementarity,
The sage chooses what is right
        without being divisive,
Points out what is true
        without being critical,
Straightens out distortions
        without overextending them,
Enlightens others without dazzling them.

其政悶悶章第五十八

Fifty-Nine

In governing people and serving heaven,
There is nothing better than thrift.

Thrift means expeditiously regaining balance
       after expending resources.
Expeditiously regaining balance
       means continually accumulating virtue.
Continually accumulating virtue
       means increasingly becoming invincible.
Increasingly becoming invincible
       means knowing that everything is possible.

One who knows that everything is possible
       is fit to govern people.
The mother principle of governing people
       holds good for a long time.
This is called deepening the root
       and firming the foundation,
Which is the way of long life and lasting vision.

治人事天章第五十九

SIXTY

Governing a big country is like cooking a small fish.
The more you stir the pot, the less the fish stays intact.

If the world is guided by the Tao,
Even evil spirits are rendered spiritless.

Not that evil spirits are in themselves spiritless,
But their spirits do not harm people.

Not only do evil spirits not harm people,
But powerful rulers also do not harm people.

When no harm is done from either side,
Virtue accrues to both
         and all return to pristine oneness.

SIXTY-ONE

A great country is like a low-lying estuary,
A place where the myriad streams of the world come together.

She is also like a receptive female drawing in an eager male.

The female always conquers the male through her stillness,
Because she knows how to lie low through her stillness.

Thus, a great country can win over a small country by lying low.
A small country can also win over a great country by lying low.

Therefore, one may either win over or be won over
      by taking the lower position.

A great country only wants
      to embrace and nourish more people.
A small country only wants
      to be embraced and serve her benefactor.

Thus, both can achieve their ends by practicing humility.
Therefore, especially a great country must practice humility.

Sixty-two

The Tao is the Innermost of all life,
The treasure of the virtuous who is centered therein,
And the refuge of the non-virtuous who has gone astray.

Beautiful words arising from the Tao
      will find an appreciative audience,
Noble deeds arising from the Tao
      will make great contributions to people,
And even if a person may have gone astray,
      the Tao will not abandon him.

Therefore, on the day a new emperor is crowned
      or new ministers installed,
Rather than rushing to offer them
      discs of jade or teams of horses,
Simply be still and show them the Tao.

Why did the ancients esteem the Tao so highly?
Did they not say that with the Tao,
Those who seek find what they seek
      and those who go astray are forgiven?

This is why the Tao is esteemed
      as the greatest treasure of the world.

道者萬物之奧章第六十二

SIXTY-THREE

Act from the still fulcrum of non-action,
Engage from the still fulcrum of non-engagement,
Experience from the still fulcrum of non-experience.

Regard the insignificant as significant,
Regard the minor as major,
Requite the unkind with kindness.

Meet the difficult while it is still easy,
Solve the major while it is still minor.
Difficult problems of the world always arise from easy ones,
Major issues of the world always arise from minor ones.

Therefore, the sage never deals with major issues,
Yet his action always leads to major accomplishment.

Those who commit lightly are seldom to be trusted.
Those who assume things to be easy
            are always met with difficulties.

Therefore, the sage assumes everything to be difficult,
And ends up having no difficulty at all.

SIXTY-FOUR

That which has balance is easy to maintain.
That which has not arisen is easy to forestall
That which is brittle is easy to shatter.
That which is minuscule is easy to scatter.
Therefore, manage problems before they arise;
Create order before disorder sets in.

A tree as large as the arms' embrace grows from a downy shoot.
A terrace nine stories high rises from a shovelful of earth.
A journey of a thousand miles begins with a single step.

One who acts from the delusion of grandiosity fails.
One who clings to the delusion of grandiosity loses.

The sage does not act from delusion,
              and therefore he does not fail,
Nor does he cling to delusion, and therefore he does not lose.

Because of the delusion of grandiosity,
On the verge of success, people often fail.
If they would take as much care at the end
              as at the beginning,
They would not fail in their affairs.

The sage does not desire what the masses desire;
He does not treasure what the masses treasure.
He studies what the masses do not study;
He returns to the source of knowledge
              ignored by the masses.

Thus, without acting in delusion,
The sage supports all beings as they naturally exist.

SIXTY-FIVE

The ancients who mastered the Tao
      did not make the people sharp and clever.
Instead, they made the people simple and deep.

The people are hard to govern
When they are too clever and know too much.

To govern the people with cleverness
      is to bring about calamities.
To govern the people with simplicity
      is to bring about blessings.

To know these two alternatives
      is to have the standard of governance.
To understand the standard of governance
      is to have sublime virtue.

Sublime virtue is deep and far-reaching.
Though it runs counter to the common way,
It follows the great way of the Tao Eternal.

古之善為道章第六十五

Sixty-six

The reason the sea is king of a hundred streams
      is because it lies below them.
Therefore, it is called king of a hundred streams.

When the sage wants to guide the people,
      in speech he always lies below them.
When the sage wants to lead the people,
      in deed he always follows behind them.

Thus, even though he is above them,
      the people do not feel oppressed.
Even though he is ahead of them,
      the people do not feel obstructed.

Therefore, the people willingly and joyously
      put him in a leadership position.
Because he is above contention,
      the people never contend with him.

江海為百谷王章第六十六

SIXTY-SEVEN

People say that my Tao is too immense and beyond compare.
However, because it is so immense, it is so different.
If it were not so different,
It would long ago have been reduced
        to something insignificant.

There are three treasures that I hold and cherish:
The first is tenderheartedness.
The second is thrift.
The third is daring not to be first in the world.

From tenderheartedness comes courage.
From thrift comes generosity.
From humility comes leadership.

If you try to be courageous
        without being tenderhearted,
If you try to be generous
        without being thrifty,
If you try to be a leader
        without learning humility,
You are courting your own self-destruction.

Venture with tenderheartedness
        and you will win the battle.
Defend with tenderheartedness
        and you will be invulnerable.
For tenderheartedness is the way
Heaven guards you for your inner protection.

天下皆謂章第六十七

90

A good warrior is never pugnacious.
A good fighter is never angry.
A good winner is never combative.
A good commander is always humble.

This is called the virtue of non-contention.
This is called using the strength of others.
This is called perfect emulation of heavenly virtue.

善為士章第六十八

SIXTY-NINE

The strategist par excellence says:
Dare not to be the aggressor but rather to be the defender.
Dare not to advance an inch but rather to retreat a foot.

This is called
Letting the opponent march
      toward nowhere to which to march,
Letting the opponent capture nothing to be captured,
Letting the opponent attack none to be attacked,
Letting the opponent arm with weapons
      for nothing for which to arm.

There is no greater calamity
      than underestimating your opponent.
To underestimate your opponent
      is surely to lose your treasures.
Therefore, when opposing forces
      are engaged in conflict,
The one who yields with caution
      will triumph in the end.

用兵有言章第六十九

SEVENTY

My words are very easy to understand
   and very easy to practice,
Yet the people of the world
   can neither understand nor practice them.

My words point to a source and my deeds a master,
Yet the people of the world
   know neither the source nor the master.

Thus, they know not who and what I am.
But for the few who know, I am precious.

Therefore, the sage may wear coarse clothes,
But will always hold a luminous treasure within.

SEVENTY-ONE

Having knowledge, yet being aware of the unknown,
      is superior intelligence.
Not having knowledge, yet pretending to know,
      is intellectual stagnation.

To be aware of stagnation is to be free of it.
The sage is free of any stagnation,
      because he is keenly aware of all stagnation.

Therefore, he is forever free of stagnation.

SEVENTY-TWO

If people do not revere the Law of Nature,
It will inexorably and adversely affect them.

If they accept it with knowledge and reverence,
It will accommodate them with balance and harmony.

Therefore, the sage, in harmony with the Law of Nature,
Knows himself but does not flaunt his knowledge,
Loves himself but does not exalt his status,
Accepts where he is without complaint,
Enjoys what he does without dislike.

Thus, he rejects imbalance and disharmony,
And chooses balance and harmony.

SEVENTY-THREE

Courage in daring action will lead to death.
Courage in caring action will lead to life.
Of these two, one is beneficial and the other harmful.

Heaven does not favor harmful courage,
Yet, there are few who really know the reason.
Thus, the sage does not make light of this truth.

He who abides by the way of Heaven
Triumphs without fighting, responds without chattering,
Reaches out without being asked,
      plans ahead without being impetuous.

Though its meshes may appear wide,
Through the vast net of heavenly law,
Nothing can ever slip.

勇於敢章第七十三

SEVENTY-FOUR

If the people do not fear death,
For reasons of extreme poverty or suffering,
What is the point of threatening them with death?

If the people fear death,
And if the outlaws are captured and killed,
Who will dare to break the law?

Yet, the act of killing should always be
The exclusive province of the Great Executioner.

Therefore, to kill in place of the Great Executioner is
Like hewing wood in place of the master carpenter;
Few, if ever, will escape cutting their own hands.

民不畏死章第七十四

SEVENTY-FIVE

Why are the people starving?
Because the rulers eat up the money in taxes.
That is why.

Why are the people difficult to govern?
Because the rulers interfere too much.
That is why.

Why do the people think so little of death?
Because the rulers think too much of their own life.
That is why.

Those who do not overvalue their life
        are wiser than those who do.

民之飢章第七十五

SEVENTY-SIX

Human beings are soft and supple at birth,
But stiff and hard at death.

All things in Nature are soft and pliant when alive,
But dry and withered when dead.

Thus, the stiff and hard is the companion of death,
And the soft and supple is the companion of life.

Therefore, an army that is unyielding will soon perish,
And a tree that is unbending will soon break.

The hard and unyielding is an inferior quality;
The soft and yielding is a superior quality.

SEVENTY-SEVEN

The Way of Heaven is like the bending of a bow.
The upper is lowered, while the lower is raised.
The too long is shortened, while the too short is lengthened.

The Way of Heaven is the way of balance:
Take from that which has more
        and give to that which has less.

The way of man is different:
Take from those who have less
        and give to those who have more.

Who is so abundant
        that he can continue to give to the world?
Only the man who embodies the Tao
        and is thus inexhaustible.

Therefore, the sage, being the fulcrum of the world,
Benefits his people without proclaiming it,
Accomplishes his task without dwelling on it,
Enlightens his world without flaunting his wisdom.

天之道章第七十七

SEVENTY-EIGHT

Nothing under heaven is as soft and yielding as water.
Yet, for attacking the hard and strong,
Nothing is better and nothing is like it.

The yielding overcomes the unyielding;
       the soft overcomes the hard.
Everyone under heaven knows this,
       yet no one puts it into practice.

Therefore, the sage says:
He who absorbs as does water the detritus of the people
       is the worthy master of the nation.
He who flows as does water
       with the tides of the troubled land
       is the worthy king of the nation.

Truth seems often paradoxical
       and against common sense.

SEVENTY-NINE

After the reconciliation of great hostilities,
Lingering resentment always remains.
Can this be considered a true reconciliation?

Therefore, the sage returns injury with kindness.
He takes the position of a giver,
And does not make claims upon others.

The virtuous relates to the world as if he owes the world.
The non-virtuous relates to the world
      as if the world owes him.

Though the way of Heaven is impartial,
It always supports those who live in harmony with it.

和大怨章第七十九

EIGHTY

Let there be small countries with few people.

Let the people take the matter of life and death seriously,
And let them not move too far from their birthplaces.

Even if there are complicated devices,
Let there be no necessity to use them.

Even if there are boats and carriages,
Let there be no reason to ride them.

Even if there are armors and weapons,
Let there be no occasion to display them.

Let the life be so simple that
The people return to tying knots for keeping records.

Let them be delighted with plain food,
      pleased with simple clothes,
      satisfied with modest homes,
      joyous with natural customs.
Though they may gaze across
      at a neighboring country,
      hearing the barking of its dogs
      and crowing of its roosters,
They are so happy and satisfied where they are
      that they will not visit one another
      until the end of their days.

小國寡民章第八十

EIGHTY-ONE

Truthful words are not always beautiful.
Beautiful words are not always truthful.

Virtuous people do not argue at all.
Non-virtuous people argue incessantly.

Those who know are not full of information.
Those who are full of information do not know.

The sage does not hoard material goods.
The more he lives entirely for others,
    the richer his life becomes.
The more he gives to others,
    the more abundant his life becomes.

The way of Heaven
    is to benefit all but to harm none.
The way of the sage
    is to work for all but to contend with none.

AFTERWORD

Herbert Guenther, Ph.D., D.Litt.

The Roman author Terentianus Maurus (late 2nd to early 3rd century CE), an authority on phonology, prosody, and meters, once stated that books' fortunes depend on their readers' capability of understanding what they have or intend to convey. His incisive observation holds as true today as it did in his time. Books highly praised today are deservedly forgotten by tomorrow, while books undeservedly consigned to oblivion have come back, vigorously alive.

One of the limited number of books that have withstood the ravages of time and continued to appeal to thinkers, be these scholars, philosophers, or others of heightened sensibilities, is the *Tao Te Ching* (nowadays officially spelled, *Daode jing*), a classic of Chinese literature. Its current name was first used by the historian Sima Qian (formerly spelled Ssu-ma Chi'en) (145-86 BCE) of the Ban dynasty (206 BCE to 220 CE). Before him it had been called Lao Tzu (Laozi) in the belief that it had been written by a person of this name, which actually is an eponym meaning the "Old One" or the "Ancient One." Another vexing problem is the fact that to this very day the authorship of this famous work has remained unresolved. There is in it no reference to other writings, persons, or events and places that might provide a clue. It was held in such high esteem that a vast number of commentaries have been written on it. Of these, more than 350 have been preserved intact in Chinese and an equal number has been lost or found only in fragments. In addition, about 250 such works are available in Japan. In passing it may be pointed out that the original work's impact on Confucianism, the once dominant thought system in the long history of China, has been enormous and without it even Chinese civilization as well as the character of the Chinese people would not have been what it was until it was overthrown and transformed in the previous century.

The word Tao (Dao) commonly means way, road, or path, but its extended meaning is principle, system, truth. Its written character consists of the radical for "going," surmounted by the character for "head," which means that the way is not an inert link between two points, but an "intelligent going." Similarly, the word Teh (De) means moral character or, as some writers prefer, virtue. Its classical Chinese definition is to "be able, to attain." In connection with Tao it means the Tao particularized as inherent in a person or thing. As such it carries with it the connotations of harmony and balance from a dynamic perspective. Consequently Taoism's much vaunted inaction (*wu-wei*) does not mean not-doing-anything. It means not interfering with the natural course (the going) the cosmos, of which we are an integral aspect, pursues of its own accord. In this spontaneousness (derived from the Latin *sponte* "of its own accord") cleans itself of its own obstructions that, with reference to the human individual, make him a "one-hundred-percenter" of his whims and prejudices, euphemistically called belief systems, ideologies, philosophies, and so on.

Of course, not everyone can read Chinese and, therefore, most readers have to rely on translations. Translating, however, *is* a tricky business, specifically, when languages (as for instance Chinese) are so different in structure from the one with which we (in the present case, English) are familiar. Moreover, any act of translating reflects on the predisposition of both the translator and the prospective reader of the translation. He/she may be a literalist concerned primarily with words and letters and less so with meanings, or he/she may be primarily concerned with meanings and connotations that have many kinds of non-literal meanings. From this it follows that a translation may be literal, but not faithful to the spirit of the text, or faithful, but not literal. In either case, each translator tries, on the basis of his/her predisposition, to convey (or impose on the reader) the kind of knowledge that he/she values most. While this observation may be construed as an axiomatic thesis of mutual exclusion, in actuality these two perspectives, which I shall call theoretical/postulational and experiential/aesthetic, intertwine and point to a common origin, which accounts for their adherents' mutual intelligibility.

Most Westerners prefer the kind of knowledge that tends to allow itself to be formally expressed in logically developed scientific or philosophical treatises and hence concerned with and based on the theoretical/postulational component in experience at the expense or disdain of the immediately experiential and aesthetic component. But what is immediately apprehended is not merely the disjunctive aggregate of inferred and postulated atoms, electrons, electromagnetic fields, and mathematical equations, but also the inspected colors, sounds, odors, flavors, and all that which we call the sensuous and sensual. These are the ingredients that make up the aesthetic component in experience. But while, for a Westerner, a rudimentary knowledge of the rules of grammar and the verbally designated relations things have to each other, suffice to understand and talk about any given topic, it is quite a different matter for an Easterner whose starting point is the aesthetic component. This, rather than being merely suggestive, must be experienced (lived through) in order to be known. What this means in particular becomes clear from the character of the Chinese language in which each immediately observed and experienced particular has its own symbol, often purely ideographic (i.e., having a directly observed form like that of what is immediately seen) and, for that reason, mostly denotative. This is one of the reasons for the fact that the Chinese language has no alphabet that, as in the case of a Western language, allows its user to produce words by merely putting together the alphabet's small number of symbols in various permutations. A direct consequence of this peculiar character of the Chinese language is its setting its individual symbols, one after the other, without any connectives between their sequence, and leaving it to the reader's imagination (not to be confused with fancying) to round out the scenery so presented. One other consequence is that the purely denotative, intuitively seen ("seen from within") and aesthetically experienced ("deeply felt") referent of a Chinese symbol with its fluidity and richness defies any facile reduction of it to the theoretically conceived and speculatively elaborated referent, superficially seen to be "out there." It would be a grave mistake to elevate these two divergent perspectives into immutable absolutes and, then, to judge them to be so. After all, when it comes to the concrete living human being, he is too much of a self-complicating complexity as to be reduced to a mere abstraction and, when it comes to him in his cultural setting, on the basis of whatever form any reductionism with its attending control and dominance psychology may assume, the literalist is as much a bore as is the aestheticist. Hence the point is to find the common ground from which the above described divergent and, in their final appearance, incompatible perspectives have evolved. This is the immediacy of experience before it becomes "channeled" into either direction.

In an environment where everything becomes politicized and, for commercial reasons, platitudinized, Yasuhiko Genku Kimura's new translation of the ancient *Tao Teh Ching* (*Daode jing*) is a notable exception. It is as clear and readable as can be wished for. On every page the reader will encounter that special and exciting glow found only when an author truly loves his subject. This engagingly written presentation is both inspiriting by letting the reader's mind soar, and restraining by not letting him lose the ground under his feet. It deserves to be read widely.

ACKNOWLEDGMENTS

Many thanks are beholden to:

Laara Lindo
    for her loving care and enduring support
    in infusing my work with beauty and poetic inspiration;
Ashok Gangadean
    for his friendship and insightful Foreword;
Herbert Guenther
    for his friendship and brilliant Afterword;
Wing Pon
    for his friendship and valued acknowledgment;
Ann Winegarden
    for her excellent editorial suggestions;
Vince Lee
    for his beautiful cover design;
Harriet Adams
    for her abiding support of and dedication to my work;
Etsuko Kimura
    for her loving care of my well-being.

As well,

Alexander Dake
    for making the publication of this book possible
    through his commitment to transforming the world
    one book at a time;
Lisa Kaiser
    for her editorial acumen and kind support
    of this translation.

About Vision-In-Action

Yasuhiko Genku Kimura is founder, chairman, and president of Vision-In-Action, the revitalization of The Twilight Club, which was originally established in the late 1870's. The original Club was a salon-type gathering of leading intellectuals, including Herbert Spencer, Ralph Waldo Emerson, Walt Whitman, Mark Twain, and Andrew Carnegie, who met regularly.

The group remained active until the 1940s with distinguished members such as IBM founder Thomas J. Watson, Sr., artist and philosopher Walter Russell, Nobel Prize winner Alexis Carrel, and others lending their support. Russell, among his other achievements, also is known for having played an important role in the famous THINK campaign at IBM, a series of lectures he delivered to employees.

Evolving from the original Twilight Club and, true to its heritage, Vision-In-Action remains a secular-based alliance of thought leaders. It develops programs that involve people from a variety of backgrounds and viewpoints in an ongoing dialogue to nurture personal and social growth.

VIA Journal
Vision-In-Action publishes a quarterly journal, VIA, edited by Yasuhiko G. Kimura. Every issue of VIA contains articles written by today's visionary thinkers and leaders.

Vision-In-Action Programs
The comprehensive Vision-In-Action programs include:
- Vision-In-Action Consortia
- Integrity in Business: Transformation of Business Culture
- Visionary Leadership Education Program
- Project Sage — A Council of Elders and Youth
- Unified Science Research and Education Program
- Project Beauty for Planetary Cultural Enrichment

Vision without Action is Empty
Action without Vision is Blind

Vision-In-Action
www.via-visioninaction.org
think@via-visioninaction.org
800.509.1955

P A R A V I E W

PARAVIEW

publishes quality works that focus on body, mind,
and spirit; the frontiers of science and culture;
and responsible business—areas related to
the transformation of society.

PARAVIEW PUBLISHING

offers books via three imprints.

PARAVIEW POCKET BOOKS
are traditionally published books co-published by
Paraview and Simon & Schuster's Pocket Books.

PARAVIEW PRESS and *PARAVIEW SPECIAL EDITIONS*
use digital print-on-demand technology to create
original paperbacks for niche audiences, as well as
reprints of previously out-of-print titles.

For a complete list of **PARAVIEW** Publishing's books
and ordering information, please visit our website at
www.paraview.com, where you can also sign up
for our free monthly media guide.

TRANSFORMING THE WORLD
ONE BOOK AT A TIME

Printed in the United States
57829LVS00009B/132

9 781931 044905